Practical
Pasta & Italian

p^3

This is a P³ Book
This edition published in 2003

P³
Queen Street House
4 Queen Street
Bath BA1 1HE, UK

ISBN: 1-40540-551-1

Printed in China

NOTE

This book uses metric and imperial measurements. Follow the same units
of measurement throughout; do not mix metric and imperial.
All spoon measurements are level: teaspoons are assumed to be 5 ml, and
tablespoons are assumed to be 15 ml. Unless otherwise stated,
milk is assumed to be full fat, eggs and individual vegetables such as potatoes
are medium, and pepper is freshly ground black pepper.

The nutritional information provided for each recipe is per serving or per person.
Optional ingredients, variations or serving suggestions have
not been included in the calculations. The times given for each recipe are an approximate
guide only because the preparation times may differ according to the techniques used by
different people and the cooking times may vary as a result of the type of oven used.

Recipes using raw or very lightly cooked eggs should be
avoided by children, the elderly, pregnant women, convalescents,
and anyone suffering from an illness.

Contents

Introduction

Pasta has existed in one form or another since the days of the Roman Empire and remains one of the most versatile ingredients in the kitchen. It can be combined with almost anything from meat to fish, vegetables to fruit, and is even delicious served with simple herb sauces. No storecupboard should be without a supply of dried pasta, which, combined with a few other stock ingredients, can be turned into a mouthwatering and nutritious meal within minutes.

Why eat pasta?

Most pasta is made from durum wheat flour and contains protein and carbohydrates. It is a good source of slow-release energy and has the additional advantage of being good value for money.

Varieties

There is an enormous range of different types of pasta, some of which are listed on the opposite page. Many are available both dried and fresh. Unless you have access to a good Italian delicatessen, it is probably not worth buying fresh, unfilled pasta, but even large stores sell high-quality tortellini, capelletti, ravioli and agnolotti. Best of all is to make fresh pasta at home. It takes a little time, but is quite easy and well worth the effort. You can mix the dough by hand or in a food processor.

Colours and flavours

Pasta may be coloured and flavoured with extra ingredients that are usually added with the beaten egg:

Black: add 1 tsp squid or cuttlefish ink.
Green: add 115 g/4 oz well-drained cooked spinach when kneading.
Purple: work 1 large, cooked beetroot in a food processor and add with an extra 60 g/2¼ oz of flour.
Red: add 2 tbsp tomato purée.

Cooking pasta

Always use a large saucepan for cooking pasta and bring lightly salted water to the boil. Add the pasta and 1 tbsp olive oil, but do not cover or the water will boil over. Quickly bring the water back to a rolling boil and avoid overcooking. When the pasta is tender, but still firm to the bite, drain and toss with butter, olive oil or your prepared sauce and serve as soon as possible.

The cooking times given here are guidelines only:

Fresh, unfilled pasta:	2–3 minutes
Fresh, filled pasta:	8–10 minutes
Dried, unfilled pasta:	10–12 minutes
Dried, filled pasta:	15–20 minutes

Basic Pasta Dough

If you wish to make your own pasta for the dishes in this book, follow this simple recipe.

SERVES 4

INGREDIENTS

450 g/1 lb durum wheat flour

4 eggs, lightly beaten

1 tbsp olive oil

salt

1 Lightly flour a work surface. Sift the flour with a pinch of salt into a mound. Make a well in the centre and add the beaten eggs and olive oil.

2 Using a fork or your fingertips, gradually work the mixture until the ingredients are combined. Knead vigorously for 10–15 minutes.

3 Set the dough aside to rest for 25 minutes, before rolling it out as thinly and evenly as possible and using as desired.

Types of pasta

There are as many as 200 different pasta shapes and about three times as many names for them. New shapes are being designed – and named – all the time and the same shape may be called a different name in different regions of Italy.

anelli, anellini: *small rings for soup*

bucatini: *long, medium-thick tubes*

cannelloni: *large, thick, round pasta tubes*

capelli d'angelo: *thin strands of 'angel hair'*

conchiglie: *ridged shells*

conchigliette: *small shells*

cresti di gallo: *curve-shaped*

ditali, ditalini: *short tubes*

eliche: *loose spirals*

farfalle: *bows*

fettucine: *medium ribbons*

fusilli: *spirals*

gemelli: *two pieces wrapped together as 'twins'*

lasagne: *flat, rectangular sheets*

linguine: *long, flat ribbons*

lumache: *snail-shaped shells*

lumaconi: *big shells*

macaroni: *long-cut or short-cut tubes*

orecchiette: *ear-shaped*

penne: *quill-shaped*

rigatoni: *thick, ridged tubes*

spaghetti: *fine or medium rods*

tagliarini: *thin ribbons*

tagliatelle: *broad ribbons*

vermicelli: *fine pasta, usually folded into skeins*

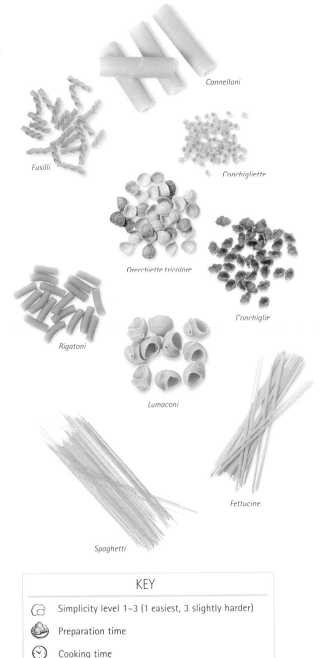

Cannelloni

Fusilli

Conchigliette

Orecchiette tricolore

Conchiglie

Rigatoni

Lumaconi

Fettucine

Spaghetti

KEY	
Simplicity level 1–3 (1 easiest, 3 slightly harder)	
Preparation time	
Cooking time	

Brown Lentil & Pasta Soup

In Italy, this soup is called *Minestrade Lentiche*. A minestra is a soup cooked with pasta; here, farfalline, a small bow-shaped variety, is used.

🍲 5 mins   🕑 25 mins

SERVES 4

INGREDIENTS

4 rashers streaky bacon, cut into small squares

1 onion, chopped

2 garlic cloves, crushed

2 celery sticks, chopped

50 g/1¾ oz farfalline or spaghetti, broken into small pieces

400 g/14 oz canned brown lentils, drained

1.2 litres/2 pints hot vegetable or ham stock

2 tbsp chopped fresh mint

1 Place the bacon in a large frying pan together with the onions, garlic, and celery. Dry fry for 4–5 minutes, stirring, until the onion is tender and the bacon is just beginning to brown.

2 Add the pasta to the frying pan and cook, stirring, for about 1 minute, to coat the pasta thoroughly in the oil.

3 Add the brown lentils and the vegetable or ham stock and bring the mixture to the boil. Lower the heat and leave to simmer for 12–15 minutes or until the pasta is tender.

4 Remove the frying pan from the heat and stir in the chopped fresh mint.

5 Transfer the soup to warm soup bowls and serve immediately.

COOK'S TIP

If you prefer to use dried lentils, add the stock before the pasta and cook for 1–1¼ hours until the lentils are tender. Add the pasta and cook for another 12–15 minutes.

Pistou

This hearty soup of beans and vegetables is from Nice and gets its name from the fresh basil sauce stirred in at the last minute.

NUTRITIONAL INFORMATION

Calories	55	Sugars	1.2g
Protein	3.8g	Fat	2.6g
Carbohydrate	4.2g	Saturates	0.6g

10 mins   25 mins

SERVES 6

INGREDIENTS

2 young carrots

450 g/1 lb potatoes

200 g/7 oz fresh peas in their shells

200 g/7 oz thin French beans

150 g/5½ oz young courgettes

2 tbsp olive oil

1 garlic clove, crushed

1 large onion, finely chopped

2.5 litres/4½ pints vegetable stock or water

1 bouquet garni, or 2 fresh parsley sprigs and 1 bay leaf tied in a 7.5-cm/3-inch piece of celery stick

85 g/3 oz dried small soup pasta

1 large tomato, skinned, deseeded and chopped or diced

freshly pared Parmesan cheese, to serve

PISTOU SAUCE

75 g/2¾ oz fresh basil leaves

1 garlic clove

5 tbsp fruity extra-virgin olive oil

salt and pepper

1. To make the pistou sauce, put the basil leaves, garlic and olive oil in a food processor and process until well blended. Season with salt and pepper to taste. Transfer to a bowl, cover with clingfilm and chill until required.

2. Peel the carrots, cut them in half lengthways then slice them. Peel the potatoes and cut into quarters lengthways, then slice. Set aside in a bowl of water until ready to use, to prevent discoloration.

3. Shell the fresh peas. Trim the French beans and cut them into 2.5-cm/1-inch pieces. Cut the courgettes in half lengthways, then slice crossways.

4. Heat the oil in a large saucepan or flameproof casserole. Add the garlic and cook for 2 minutes, stirring. Add the onion and continue cooking for 2 minutes until soft. Add the carrots and potatoes and stir for about 30 seconds.

5. Pour in the stock and bring to the boil. Lower the heat, partially cover and simmer for 8 minutes until the vegetables are starting to become tender.

6. Stir in the peas, beans, courgettes, bouquet garni, pasta and tomato. Season and cook for 4 minutes or until the vegetables and pasta are tender. Stir in the pistou sauce and serve with Parmesan.

Lemon & Chicken Soup

This delicately flavoured summer soup is surprisingly easy to make and tastes absolutely delicious.

NUTRITIONAL INFORMATION

Calories 506   Sugars 4g
Protein .... 19g   Fat 31g
Carbohydrate ... 41g   Saturates 19g

5–10 mins   1¼ hrs

SERVES 4

INGREDIENTS

4 tbsp butter

8 shallots, thinly sliced

2 carrots, thinly sliced

2 celery sticks, thinly sliced

225 g/8 oz boned chicken breasts, finely chopped

3 lemons

1.2 litres/2 pints chicken stock

225 g/8 oz dried spaghetti, broken into small pieces

150 ml/5 fl oz double cream

salt and white pepper

TO GARNISH

sprigs of fresh parsley

fresh lemon slices, halved

1 Melt the butter in a large saucepan. Add the shallots, carrots, celery and chicken and cook over a low heat, stirring occasionally, for 8 minutes.

2 Thinly pare the lemons and then blanch the zest in boiling water for 3 minutes. Squeeze the juice from the lemons.

3 Add the lemon rind and juice and the chicken stock to the pan. Bring slowly to the boil over a low heat. Simmer for 40 minutes, stirring occasionally.

4 Add the spaghetti to the pan and cook for 15 minutes. Season to taste with salt and white pepper and add the cream. Heat through, but do not let the soup boil or it will curdle.

5 Pour the soup into a large serving bowl or individual soup bowls, garnish with sprigs of parsley and half slices of lemon and serve immediately.

COOK'S TIP

You can prepare this soup up to the end of step 3 in advance, so that all you need do before serving is heat it through before adding the pasta and the finishing touches.

Spinach & Herb Orzo

Serve this vibrant green pasta dish with any grilled meat or seafood.
Orzo, shaped like grains of barley, is popular in southern Italy and Greece.

NUTRITIONAL INFORMATION

Calories 304	Sugars 8g	
Protein 12g	Fat 6g	
Carbohydrate . . . 54g	Saturates 1g	

15–20 mins   10 mins

SERVES 4

INGREDIENTS

1 tsp salt

250 g/9 oz dried orzo

200 g/7 oz baby spinach leaves

150 g/5½ oz rocket

25 g/1 oz fresh flat-leaved parsley

25 g/1 oz fresh coriander

4 spring onions

2 tbsp extra-virgin olive oil

1 tbsp garlic-flavoured olive oil

pepper

TO SERVE

radicchio or other lettuce leaves

55 g/2 oz feta cheese, well drained and
   crumbled (optional)

lemon slices

1 Bring 2 pans of water to the boil, and put 12 ice cubes in a bowl of cold water. Add the salt and orzo to one of the pans, return to the boil and cook for about 8–10 minutes, or according to packet instructions, until the pasta is tender.

2 Meanwhile, remove any tough spinach stems. Rinse the leaves to remove any grit. Chop the rocket, parsley, coriander and green parts of the spring onions.

3 Put the spinach, rocket, parsley, coriander and spring onions in the other pan of boiling water and blanch for 15 seconds. Drain and transfer to the iced water to preserve the colour.

4 When the spinach, herbs and spring onions are cool, squeeze out all the excess water. Transfer to a small food processor and process. Add the olive oil and garlic-flavoured oil and process again until the spinach mixture is well blended.

5 Drain the orzo well and stir in the spinach mixture. Toss well and adjust the seasoning.

6 Line a serving platter with radicchio leaves and pile the orzo on top. Sprinkle with feta cheese, if desired, and garnish with lemon slices. Serve hot or leave to cool to room temperature.

Filled Aubergines

Combined with tomatoes and melting mozzarella cheese, pasta makes a tasty filling for baked aubergine shells.

NUTRITIONAL INFORMATION

Calories 342   Sugars 6g
Protein . . . . 11g   Fat 16g
Carbohydrate . . . 40g   Saturates 4g

🍰 25 mins   🕐 55 mins

SERVES 4

I N G R E D I E N T S

225 g/8 oz dried penne or other short
   pasta shapes

4 tbsp olive oil, plus extra for brushing

2 aubergines

1 large onion, chopped

2 garlic cloves, crushed

400 g/14 oz canned chopped tomatoes

2 tsp dried oregano

55 g/2 oz mozzarella cheese, thinly sliced

25 g/1 oz Parmesan cheese, freshly grated

2 tbsp dried breadcrumbs

salt and pepper

salad leaves, to serve

1 Bring a large saucepan of lightly salted water to the boil. Add the pasta and 1 tablespoon of the olive oil, bring back to the boil and then cook for 8–10 minutes or until tender but still firm to the bite. Drain, return to the pan, cover and keep warm.

2 Cut the aubergines in half lengthways and score around the insides with a sharp knife, being careful not to pierce the shells. Scoop out the flesh with a spoon. Brush the insides of the shells with olive oil. Chop the flesh and set aside.

3 Heat the remaining oil in a frying pan. Cook the onion until translucent. Add the garlic and cook for 1 minute, then add the chopped aubergine and cook, stirring frequently, for 5 minutes.

4 Add the chopped tomatoes and dried oregano to the pan, and season to taste with salt and pepper. Bring the mixture to the boil, then lower the heat and simmer for 10 minutes or until it has thickened. Remove the pan from the heat and stir in the pasta.

5 Brush a baking tray with oil and arrange the aubergine shells in a single layer. Divide half of the tomato and pasta mixture between them. Scatter over the mozzarella slices, then pile the remaining tomato and pasta mixture on top. Mix the Parmesan and breadcrumbs and sprinkle over, pressing lightly into the mixture.

6 Bake in a preheated oven, 200°C/ 400°F/Gas Mark 6, for 25 minutes or until the topping is golden brown. Serve hot with mixed salad leaves.

Pasta Omelette

This is a superb way of using up any leftover pasta, such as penne, macaroni or conchiglie.

NUTRITIONAL INFORMATION

Calories	638	Sugars	5g
Protein	24g	Fat	38g
Carbohydrate	53g	Saturates	7g

5 mins   15–20 mins

SERVES 2

INGREDIENTS

4 tbsp olive oil

1 small onion, chopped

1 fennel bulb, thinly sliced

125 g/4½ oz potato, diced

1 garlic clove, chopped

4 eggs

1 tbsp chopped fresh flat-leaved parsley

pinch of chilli powder

100 g/3½ oz cooked short pasta

2 tbsp stuffed green olives, halved

salt and pepper

sprigs of fresh marjoram, to garnish

tomato salad, to serve

1 Heat half the oil in a heavy-based frying pan over a low heat. Add the onion, fennel and potato and cook, stirring occasionally, for 8–10 minutes until the potato is just tender.

2 Stir in the chopped garlic and cook for 1 minute. Remove the pan from the heat, transfer the vegetables to a plate and set aside to keep warm.

3 Beat the eggs until they are frothy. Stir in the parsley and season with salt, pepper and a pinch of chilli powder.

4 Heat 1 tablespoon of the remaining oil in a clean frying pan. Add half of the egg mixture to the pan, then add the cooked vegetables, pasta and half of the olives. Pour in the remaining egg mixture and cook until the sides begin to set.

5 Lift up the edges of the omelette with a palette knife to allow the uncooked egg to spread underneath. Cook, shaking the pan occasionally, until the underside of the omelette is a light golden-brown colour.

6 Slide the omelette out of the pan onto a plate. Wipe the pan with kitchen paper and heat the remaining oil. Invert the omelette into the pan and cook until the other side is golden brown.

7 Slide the omelette onto a warmed serving dish and garnish with the remaining olives and the marjoram. Serve cut into wedges, with a tomato salad.

Cheese, Nut & Pasta Salad

Use colourful salad leaves to provide visual contrast to complement the variations in taste and texture.

NUTRITIONAL INFORMATION

Calories . . . . 694 Sugars 1g
Protein . . . . 22g Fat 57g
Carbohydrate . . . 24g Saturates 15g

15 mins   15–20 mins

SERVES 4

I N G R E D I E N T S

225 g/8 oz dried pasta shells

1 tbsp olive oil

115 g/4 oz shelled and halved walnuts

mixed salad leaves, such as radicchio, escarole, rocket, lamb's lettuce and frisée

225 g/8 oz dolcelatte cheese, crumbled

salt

D R E S S I N G

2 tbsp walnut oil

4 tbsp extra-virgin olive oil

2 tbsp red wine vinegar

salt and pepper

1 Bring a pan of lightly salted water to the boil. Add the pasta and olive oil and cook for 8–10 minutes or until tender but firm to the bite. Drain, refresh under cold running water, drain again and set aside.

2 Spread out the shelled walnut halves onto a baking tray and toast under a preheated grill for 2–3 minutes. Set aside to cool while you make the dressing.

3 To make the dressing, whisk together the walnut oil, olive oil and vinegar in a small bowl and season to taste.

4 Arrange the salad leaves in a large serving bowl. Pile the cooled pasta in the middle of the salad leaves and sprinkle over the dolcelatte cheese. Just before serving, pour the dressing over the pasta salad, scatter over the walnut halves and toss together to mix and to coat in the dressing. Serve immediately.

COOK'S TIP

Dolcelatte is a semi-soft, blue-veined cheese from Italy. Its texture is creamy and smooth and the flavour is delicate, but piquant. You could use Roquefort instead. It is essential that whatever cheese you choose, it is of the best quality and in peak condition.

Garlic Mushroom Pizza

This pizza dough is flavoured with garlic and herbs and topped with mixed mushrooms and melting cheese for a really delicious pizza.

NUTRITIONAL INFORMATION

Calories 541   Sugars 5g
Protein . . . . .16g   Fat 15g
Carbohydrate . . .91g   Saturates 6g

45 mins   30 mins

SERVES 4

I N G R E D I E N T S

D O U G H

450 g/1 lb strong white flour, plus extra
    for dusting

2 tsp easy-blend dried yeast

2 garlic cloves, crushed

2 tbsp chopped fresh thyme

2 tbsp olive oil, plus extra for greasing

300 ml/10 fl oz lukewarm water

T O P P I N G

2 tbsp butter or margarine

350 g/12 oz mixed mushrooms, sliced

2 garlic cloves, crushed

2 tbsp chopped fresh parsley, plus extra
    to garnish

2 tbsp tomato purée

6 tbsp passata

85 g/3 oz mozzarella cheese, grated

salt and pepper

1 Mix the flour, yeast, garlic and thyme in a bowl. Make a well in the centre and gradually stir in the oil and water. Bring together to form a soft dough.

2 Turn the dough onto a floured work surface and knead for 5 minutes or until smooth. Roll into a 35-cm/14-inch circle. Brush a baking tray with a little oil and place the dough base on it. Set aside in a warm place for about 20 minutes or until the dough puffs up.

3 Meanwhile, make the topping. Melt the butter or margarine in a frying pan and cook the mushrooms, garlic and parsley over a low heat for 5 minutes.

4 Combine the tomato purée and passata and spoon onto the pizza base, leaving a 1-cm/½-inch border of dough. Spoon the mushroom mixture on top. Season to taste with salt and pepper and sprinkle over the cheese.

5 Cook the pizza in a preheated oven, 190°C/375°F/Gas Mark 5 for 20–25 minutes or until the base is crisp and the cheese has melted. Garnish with chopped parsley and serve the pizza immediately.

Patriotic Pasta

The ingredients of this dish have the same bright colours as the Italian flag – hence its name.

NUTRITIONAL INFORMATION

Calories 325	Sugars 5g
Protein 8g	Fat 13g
Carbohydrate ... 48g	Saturates 2g

5 mins   15 mins

SERVES 4

I N G R E D I E N T S

450 g/1 lb dried farfalle

4 tbsp olive oil

450 g/1 lb cherry tomatoes

90 g/3¼ oz rocket

salt and pepper

pecorino cheese, to garnish

1 Bring a large saucepan of lightly salted water to the boil. Add the farfalle and 1 tablespoon of the olive oil and cook for 8–10 minutes or until tender but still firm to the bite. Drain the farfalle thoroughly and return to the pan.

2 Cut the cherry tomatoes in half and trim the rocket.

3 Heat the remaining olive oil in a large saucepan. Add the tomatoes to the pan and cook for 1 minute. Add the farfalle and rocket to the pan and stir gently to mix. Heat the mixture through and season to taste with salt and pepper.

4 Meanwhile, using a vegetable peeler, shave thin slices of pecorino cheese.

5 Transfer the farfalle and vegetables to a warm serving dish. Garnish with the cheese shavings and serve immediately.

COOK'S TIP
Pecorino cheese is a hard sheep's milk cheese that resembles Parmesan, and is often used for grating over a variety of dishes. It has a mature flavour and is only used in small quantities.

Vegetable Pasta Nests

These large pasta nests look impressive when presented filled with grilled mixed vegetables, and taste delicious.

NUTRITIONAL INFORMATION

Calories 392   Sugars 1g
Protein .... 6g   Fat 28g
Carbohydrate ... 32g   Saturates 9g

25 mins   40 mins

SERVES 4

I N G R E D I E N T S

175 g/6 oz spaghetti

1 aubergine, halved and sliced

1 courgette, diced

1 red pepper, deseeded and sliced
   diagonally

6 tbsp olive oil

2 garlic cloves, crushed

4 tbsp butter or margarine, melted

1 tbsp dried white breadcrumbs

salt and pepper

sprigs of fresh parsley, to garnish

1 Bring a large saucepan of water to the boil. Add the spaghetti and cook for 8–10 minutes or until tender but still firm to the bite. Drain the spaghetti and set aside until required.

2 Place the aubergine, courgette and red pepper on a baking tray. Mix the oil and garlic together and pour over the vegetables, brushing to coat all over.

3 Cook the vegetables under a preheated hot grill for about 10 minutes, turning, until tender and lightly charred. Set aside and keep warm.

4 Divide the spaghetti among 4 large cups of a lightly greased muffin tin. Using 2 forks, arrange it to form nests.

5 Brush the pasta nests with melted butter or margarine and sprinkle with breadcrumbs. Bake in a preheated oven, 200°C/400°F/Gas Mark 6, for 15 minutes or until lightly golden. Remove the nests from the pans and transfer to serving plates. Divide the vegetables between the nests, season and garnish with parsley sprigs.

Green Tagliatelle with Garlic

A rich pasta dish for garlic lovers everywhere. It is quick and easy to prepare, and full of flavour.

NUTRITIONAL INFORMATION

Calories 526	Sugars 3g	
Protein 14g	Fat 34g	
Carbohydrate ... 45g	Saturates 13g	

5 mins   20 mins

SERVES 4

I N G R E D I E N T S

2 tbsp walnut oil

1 bunch spring onions, sliced

2 garlic cloves, thinly sliced

250 g/9 oz mushrooms, sliced

450 g/1 lb fresh green and white tagliatelle

1 tbsp olive oil

225 g/8 oz frozen spinach, thawed
and drained

115 g/4 oz full-fat soft cheese with garlic
and herbs

4 tbsp single cream

60 g/2¼ oz unsalted pistachio nuts, chopped

2 tbsp shredded fresh basil

salt and pepper

sprigs of fresh basil, to garnish

fresh Italian bread, to serve

3 Meanwhile, bring a large saucepan of lightly salted water to the boil. Add the tagliatelle and olive oil and cook for 3–5 minutes or until tender but still firm to the bite. Drain the tagliatelle thoroughly and return to the pan.

4 Add the spinach to the frying pan and heat through for 1–2 minutes. Add the cheese to the frying pan and let it melt slightly. Stir in the cream and continue to cook, without letting the mixture boil, until warmed through.

5 Pour the sauce over the pasta, season to taste with salt and black pepper and mix well. Heat through gently, stirring constantly, for 2–3 minutes.

6 Transfer the pasta to a serving dish and sprinkle over the pistachio nuts and shredded basil. Garnish with the basil sprigs and serve immediately with the Italian bread of your choice.

1 Heat the walnut oil in a large frying pan. Add the spring onions and garlic and fry for 1 minute until just softened.

2 Add the mushrooms to the pan, stir well, cover and cook over a low heat for about 5 minutes until softened.

Spinach & Nut Pasta

Use any pasta shapes that you have for this recipe. Multicoloured pasta is visually the most attractive.

NUTRITIONAL INFORMATION

Calories	603	Sugars	5g
Protein	12g	Fat	41g
Carbohydrate	46g	Saturates	6g

5 mins   15 mins

SERVES 4

INGREDIENTS

225 g/8 oz dried pasta shapes

125 ml/4 fl oz olive oil

2 garlic cloves, crushed

1 onion, cut into quarters and sliced

3 large flat mushrooms, sliced

225 g/8 oz spinach

2 tbsp pine kernels

6 tbsp dry white wine

salt and pepper

Parmesan shavings, to garnish

1 Cook the pasta in a saucepan of boiling salted water for 8–10 minutes or until tender but still firm to the bite. Drain well.

2 Meanwhile, heat the oil in a large saucepan and cook the crushed garlic and sliced onion for 1 minute.

3 Add the sliced mushrooms to the pan and cook over a medium heat, stirring occasionally, for 2 minutes.

4 Lower the heat, add the spinach to the pan and cook, stirring occasionally, for 4–5 minutes or until it has wilted.

5 Stir in the pine kernels and wine, season to taste and cook for 1 minute.

6 Transfer the pasta to a warm serving bowl and toss the sauce into it, mixing well. Garnish with shavings of Parmesan cheese and serve.

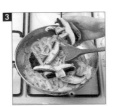

COOK'S TIP
Nutmeg has a particular affinity with spinach, so grate a little over this dish to give it extra flavour.

Spinach & Mushroom Lasagne

This is an extremely tasty vegetarian dish. For a variation you could substitute sliced roasted peppers for the spinach (see below).

NUTRITIONAL INFORMATION

Calories	720	Sugars	9g
Protein	31g	Fat	52g
Carbohydrate	36g	Saturates	32g

20 mins 40 mins

SERVES 4

I N G R E D I E N T S

115 g/4 oz butter, plus extra for greasing

2 garlic cloves, finely chopped

115 g/4 oz shallots

225 g/8 oz wild mushrooms, such as chanterelles

450 g/1 lb spinach, cooked, drained and finely chopped

225 g/8 oz Cheddar cheese, grated

¼ tsp freshly grated nutmeg

1 tsp chopped fresh basil

55 g/2 oz plain flour

600 ml/1 pint hot milk

60 g/2¼ oz Cheshire cheese, grated

8 sheets precooked lasagne

salt and pepper

1 Lightly grease a large ovenproof dish with a little butter.

2 Melt half of the butter in a saucepan. Add the garlic, shallots and mushrooms and cook over a low heat for 3 minutes. Stir in the spinach, Cheddar cheese, nutmeg and basil. Season with salt and pepper to taste and set aside.

3 Melt the remaining butter in another saucepan over a low heat. Add the flour and cook, stirring constantly, for 1 minute. Gradually stir in the hot milk,

whisking constantly, until smooth. Stir in 25 g/1 oz of the Cheshire cheese and season to taste with salt and pepper.

4 Spread half of the mushroom and spinach mixture over the bottom of the prepared dish. Cover with a layer of lasagne, then with half of the cheese sauce. Repeat the process and sprinkle over the remaining Cheshire cheese.

5 Bake in a preheated oven, 200°C/400°F/ Gas Mark 6, for 30 minutes or until golden brown. Serve the lasagne very hot.

VARIATION

You could substitute 4 peppers for the spinach. Roast the peppers in a preheated oven, 200°C/400°F/Gas Mark 6, for 20 minutes. Rub off the skins under cold water, deseed and chop before using.

Pasta & Vegetable Sauce

The shapes and textures of the vegetables make a mouthwatering presentation in this light and summery dish.

NUTRITIONAL INFORMATION

Calories 389	Sugars 4g	
Protein 16g	Fat 20g	
Carbohydrate ... 38g	Saturates 11g	

10 mins 30 mins

SERVES 4

INGREDIENTS

225 g/8 oz dried gemelli or other pasta shapes

1 tbsp olive oil

1 head green broccoli, cut into florets

2 courgettes, sliced

225 g/8 oz asparagus spears

115 g/4 oz mangetouts

115 g/4 oz frozen peas

2 tbsp butter

3 tbsp vegetable stock

4 tbsp double cream

freshly grated nutmeg

2 tbsp chopped fresh parsley

2 tbsp freshly grated Parmesan cheese

salt and pepper

1 Bring a large saucepan of lightly salted water to the boil. Add the pasta and olive oil and cook for 8–10 minutes or until tender but still firm to the bite. Drain, return to the pan, cover and keep warm.

2 Steam the broccoli, courgettes, asparagus spears and mangetouts over a pan of boiling salted water until they are just beginning to soften, then remove from the heat and refresh in cold water. Drain and set aside.

3 Bring a small saucepan of lightly salted water to the boil. Add the frozen peas and cook for 3 minutes. Drain the peas, refresh in cold water then drain again. Set aside with the other vegetables.

4 Melt the butter with the vegetable stock in a pan over a medium heat. Add all the vegetables, reserving a few of the asparagus spears, and toss carefully with a wooden spoon until they have heated through, taking care not to break them up.

5 Stir in the cream and heat through without bringing to the boil. Season to taste with salt, pepper, and nutmeg.

6 Transfer the pasta to a warmed serving dish and stir in the chopped parsley. Spoon over the vegetable sauce and sprinkle over the Parmesan cheese. Arrange the reserved asparagus spears in a pattern on top and serve.

Fettucine all'Alfredo

This simple, traditional dish can be made with any long pasta, but is especially good with flat noodles, such as fettucine or tagliatelle.

NUTRITIONAL INFORMATION

Calories	540	Sugars	2g
Protein	15g	Fat	40g
Carbohydrate	31g	Saturates	23g

5 mins   5 mins

SERVES 4

INGREDIENTS

2 tbsp butter

200 ml/7 fl oz double cream

450 g/1 lb fresh fettucine

1 tbsp olive oil

90 g/3¼ oz Parmesan cheese, freshly grated, plus extra to serve

pinch of freshly grated nutmeg

salt and pepper

sprigs of fresh flat-leaved parsley, to garnish

2 Meanwhile, bring a large saucepan of lightly salted water to the boil. Add the fettucine and olive oil and cook for 2–3 minutes or until tender but still firm to the bite. Drain the fettucine thoroughly and return it to the warm pan, then pour over the cream sauce.

3 Toss the fettucine in the sauce over a low heat until thoroughly coated.

4 Add the remaining cream and the Parmesan cheese and nutmeg to the fettucine mixture, and season to taste with salt and pepper. Toss thoroughly to coat while gently heating through.

5 Transfer the fettucine to a warm serving plate and garnish with fresh parsley. Serve immediately, handing extra grated Parmesan cheese separately.

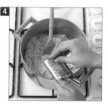

1 Put the butter and 150 ml/5 fl oz of the cream in a large saucepan and bring the mixture to the boil over a medium heat. Lower the heat and simmer gently for about 1½ minutes or until slightly thickened.

VARIATION

This classic Roman dish is often served with the addition of strips of ham and fresh peas. Add 225 g/8oz shelled cooked peas and 175 g/6 oz ham strips with the Parmesan cheese in step 4.

Italian Fish Stew

This robust stew is full of Mediterranean flavours. If you do not want to prepare the fish yourself, ask your local fishmonger to do it for you.

NUTRITIONAL INFORMATION

Calories 236   Sugars 4g
Protein . . . . 20g   Fat 7g
Carbohydrate . . . 25g   Saturates 1g

5–10 mins   25 mins

SERVES 4

INGREDIENTS

2 tbsp olive oil

2 red onions, finely chopped

1 garlic clove, crushed

2 courgettes, sliced

400 g/14 oz canned chopped tomatoes

850 ml/1½ pints vegetable or fish stock

90 g/3¼ oz dried pasta shapes

350 g/12 oz firm white fish, such as cod, haddock or hake

1 tbsp chopped fresh basil or oregano, or 1 tsp dried oregano

1 tsp grated lemon zest

1 tbsp cornflour

1 tbsp water

salt and pepper

sprigs of fresh basil or oregano, to garnish

3 Skin and bone the fish, then cut it into chunks. Add the fish chunks to the pan with the herbs and lemon zest and cook gently for 5 minutes until the fish is opaque and flakes easily (take care not to overcook it).

4 Blend the cornflour with the water and stir into the stew. Cook gently for 2 minutes, stirring, until thickened. Season with salt and pepper to taste and ladle into warmed soup bowls. Garnish with sprigs of basil or oregano and serve at once.

1 Heat the oil in a large saucepan and then cook the onions and garlic for 5 minutes. Add the courgettes and continue to cook for 2–3 minutes, stirring often.

2 Add the tomatoes and stock to the pan and bring to the boil. Add the pasta, cover the pan and lower the heat. Simmer for 5 minutes.

Smoked Haddock Casserole

This quick, easy and inexpensive dish would be ideal for a midweek family supper.

NUTRITIONAL INFORMATION

Calories	525	Sugars	........8g
Protein	........41g	Fat	..........18g
Carbohydrate	...53g	Saturates	......10g

🍥 🍥 🍥

🍰 20 mins   🕐 45 mins

SERVES 4

INGREDIENTS

2 tbsp butter, plus extra for greasing

450 g/1 lb smoked haddock fillets, cut into 4 slices

600 ml/1 pint milk

2 tbsp plain flour

pinch of freshly grated nutmeg

3 tbsp double cream

1 tbsp chopped fresh parsley

2 eggs, hard-boiled and mashed to a pulp

450 g/1 lb dried fusilli

1 tbsp lemon juice

salt and pepper

cooked new potatoes and beetroot, to serve

1 Thoroughly grease a casserole dish with butter. Put the haddock in the casserole and pour over the milk. Bake in a preheated oven, 200°C/400°F/Gas Mark 6, for about 15 minutes. Carefully pour the cooking liquid into a jug without breaking up the fish.

2 Melt the 2 tablespoons of butter in a saucepan and stir in the flour. Gradually whisk in the reserved cooking liquid. Season to taste with salt, pepper and nutmeg. Stir in the cream, parsley and mashed eggs and cook, stirring constantly, for 2 minutes.

3 Meanwhile, bring a large saucepan of lightly salted water to the boil. Add the fusilli and lemon juice and cook for 8-10 minutes until tender but still firm to the bite.

4 Drain the pasta and spoon or tip it over the fish. Top with the egg sauce and return the casserole to the oven for another 10 minutes.

5 Serve the fish casserole with boiled new potatoes and freshly cooked beetroot.

VARIATION

You can use any type of dried pasta for this casserole. Try penne, conchiglie or rigatoni.

Fillets of Red Mullet & Pasta

In this recipe, a lemon and herb sauce perfectly complements the sweet flavour and delicate texture of the fish.

NUTRITIONAL INFORMATION

Calories 457   Sugars 3g
Protein .... 39g   Fat 12g
Carbohydrate ... 44g   Saturates 5g

15 mins   1 hr

SERVES 4

INGREDIENTS

1 kg/2 lb 4 oz red mullet fillets

300 ml/10 fl oz dry white wine

4 shallots, finely chopped

1 garlic clove, crushed

3 tbsp finely chopped fresh mixed herbs

finely grated zest and juice of 1 lemon

pinch of freshly grated nutmeg

3 anchovy fillets, roughly chopped

1 tbsp butter

2 tbsp double cream

1 tsp cornflour

450 g/1 lb dried vermicelli

1 tbsp olive oil

salt and pepper

TO GARNISH

sprig of fresh mint

lemon slices

lemon zest

1 Put the red mullet fillets in a large casserole. Pour over the wine and add half the chopped shallots with the garlic, herbs, lemon zest and juice, nutmeg and anchovies. Season, cover the casserole and bake in a preheated oven, 180°C/350°F/Gas Mark 4, for 35 minutes.

2 Carefully lift out the baked fish and transfer to a warm plate. Set the plate aside and keep warm. Strain and reserve the cooking liquid.

3 Heat the butter in a pan and cook the remaining shallots over a low heat, stirring, for 5 minutes. Pour the cooking liquid into the pan and bring to the boil. Simmer for 25 minutes until reduced by half. Mix the cream and cornflour together and stir into the sauce to thicken.

4 Meanwhile, bring a saucepan of lightly salted water to the boil. Add the vermicelli and oil and cook for 8–10 minutes or until tender but still firm to the bite. Drain the pasta and transfer to a warm serving dish.

5 Arrange the fish fillets on top of the vermicelli and pour over the sauce. Garnish with a fresh mint sprig, slices of lemon and strips of lemon zest, and serve immediately.

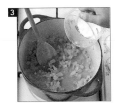

Seafood Lasagne

You can use any fish and any sauce you like in this recipe: try smoked haddock and whisky sauce, or cod with cheese sauce.

NUTRITIONAL INFORMATION

Calories	....	790	Sugars 23g
Protein	....	55g	Fat 32g
Carbohydrate	...	74g	Saturates 19g

30 mins   45 mins

SERVES 4

INGREDIENTS

450 g/1 lb smoked haddock, filleted, skin removed and flesh flaked

115 g/4 oz prawns, peeled and deveined

115 g/4 oz sole fillet, skin removed and flesh sliced

juice of 1 lemon

SAUCE

4 tbsp butter

3 leeks, very thinly sliced

60 g/2¼ oz plain flour

600 ml/1 pint milk

2 tbsp clear honey

200 g/7 oz mozzarella cheese, grated

450 g/1 lb pre-cooked lasagne

60 g/2¼ oz Parmesan cheese, freshly grated

pepper

VARIATION

For a cider sauce, substitute 1 finely chopped shallot for the leeks, 300 ml/10 fl oz cider and 300 ml/10 fl oz double cream for the milk, and 1 teaspoon of mustard for the honey. For a Tuscan sauce, substitute 1 chopped fennel bulb for the leeks, and omit the honey.

1 Put the haddock fillet, prawns and sole fillet into a large bowl, season with pepper and add lemon juice to taste. Cover the bowl and set it aside while you make the sauce.

2 Melt the butter in a large saucepan. Add the leeks and cook, stirring occasionally, for 8 minutes. Add the flour and cook, stirring constantly, for 1 minute. Gradually stir in enough milk to make a thick, creamy sauce.

3 Stir in the honey and mozzarella cheese and continue cooking for another 3 minutes. Remove the pan from the heat and mix in the fish and prawns.

4 Arrange alternate layers of fish sauce and lasagne in an ovenproof dish, finishing with a fish sauce layer on top. Sprinkle over the grated Parmesan cheese. Bake in a preheated oven, 180°C/350°F/Gas Mark 4, for 30 minutes. Remove from the oven and serve immediately.

Linguine with Sardines

This is a very quick dish that is ideal for midweek suppers because it is so simple to prepare yet full of flavour.

NUTRITIONAL INFORMATION

Calories	547	Sugars	5g
Protein	23g	Fat	23g
Carbohydrate	68g	Saturates	3g

5–10 mins   10–15 mins

SERVES 4

INGREDIENTS

8 sardines, filleted

1 fennel bulb

4 tbsp olive oil

3 garlic cloves, sliced

1 tsp chilli flakes

350 g/12 oz dried linguine

½ tsp finely grated lemon zest

1 tbsp lemon juice

2 tbsp pine kernels, toasted

2 tbsp chopped fresh parsley, plus extra to garnish

salt and pepper

1 Wash and dry the sardines. Roughly chop them into large pieces and set aside. Trim the fennel bulb, removing any tough outer leaves, and slice very thinly.

2 Heat 2 tablespoons of the olive oil in a large frying pan and add the garlic and chilli flakes. Cook for 1 minute then add the fennel. Cook over a medium-high heat for 4–5 minutes until softened. Add the sardine pieces and heat for another 3–4 minutes until just cooked.

3 Meanwhile, cook the pasta in plenty of boiling salted water according to the packet instructions, until tender but still firm to the bite. Drain well and return to the pan to keep warm.

4 Add the lemon zest and juice, pine kernels, parsley and seasoning to the sardines and toss together. Add the mixture to the pasta with the remaining olive oil and toss together gently. Serve immediately with a sprinkling of parsley.

COOK'S TIP

Reserve a couple of tablespoons of the pasta cooking water and add it to the pasta with the sauce if the mixture seems a little dry.

Tagliatelle with Pumpkin

This unusual dish comes from the Emilia Romagna region. Why not serve it with Lambrusco, the local wine?

NUTRITIONAL INFORMATION

Calories .... 559 Sugars 7g
Protein .... 17g   Fat 32g
Carbohydrate ... 55g Saturates 14g

5 mins   20–25 mins

SERVES 4

I N G R E D I E N T S

500 g/1 lb 2 oz pumpkin or butternut
  squash, peeled and deseeded

3 tbsp olive oil

1 onion, finely chopped

2 garlic cloves, crushed

4–6 tbsp chopped fresh parsley

pinch of freshly grated nutmeg

250 ml/9 fl oz vegetable or chicken stock

115 g/4 oz Parma ham, cut into small pieces

250 g/9 oz dried tagliatelle

150 ml/5 fl oz double cream

salt and pepper

freshly grated Parmesan cheese, to serve

1 Cut the pumpkin or butternut squash in half and scoop out the seeds with a spoon. Cut the pumpkin or squash into 1-cm/½-inch cubes.

2 Heat 2 tablespoons of the olive oil in a large saucepan. Add the onion and garlic and cook over a low heat for about 3 minutes until soft. Add half the parsley and cook for 1 minute.

3 Add the pumpkin pieces and cook for 2–3 minutes. Season to taste with salt, pepper and nutmeg.

4 Add half the stock to the pan, bring to the boil, cover and simmer for about 10 minutes or until the pumpkin is tender. Add more stock if the pumpkin is becoming dry and looks as if it might be about to burn.

5 Add the Parma ham to the pan and cook, stirring, for another 2 minutes.

6 Meanwhile, bring a large saucepan of lightly salted water to the boil. Add the tagliatelle and the remaining oil and cook for 12 minutes or until tender but still firm to the bite. Drain the pasta and transfer to a warm serving dish.

7 Stir the cream into the pumpkin and Parma ham mixture and heat through well. Spoon the pumpkin mixture over the tagliatelle, sprinkle over the remaining parsley and serve while still hot. Hand the grated Parmesan separately.

Chicken Suprême Spaghetti

The refreshing combination of chicken and orange sauce makes this a perfect dish for a warm summer evening.

NUTRITIONAL INFORMATION

Calories	933	Sugars	34g
Protein	74g	Fat	24g
Carbohydrate	100g	Saturates	5g

5 mins   25 mins

SERVES 4

INGREDIENTS

2 tbsp rapeseed oil

3 tbsp olive oil

4 chicken suprêmes, about 225 g/8 oz each

150 ml/5 fl oz orange brandy

2 tbsp plain flour

150 ml/5 fl oz freshly squeezed orange juice

25 g/1 oz courgette, cut into very thin strips

25 g/1 oz leek, finely shredded

25 g/1 oz red pepper, cut into very thin strips

400 g/14 oz dried wholemeal spaghetti

3 large oranges, peeled and cut into segments

rind of 1 orange, cut into very thin strips

2 tbsp chopped fresh tarragon

150 g/5½ oz fromage frais or ricotta cheese

salt and pepper

fresh tarragon leaves, to garnish

1 Heat the rapeseed oil and 1 tablespoon of the olive oil in a frying pan. Add the chicken and cook quickly until golden brown. Add the orange brandy and cook for 3 minutes. Sprinkle over the flour and cook for 2 minutes.

2 Lower the heat and add the orange juice, courgette, leek and red pepper and season with salt and pepper. Simmer for 5 minutes until the sauce has thickened.

3 Meanwhile, bring a pan of salted water to the boil. Add the spaghetti and 1 tablespoon of the olive oil and cook for 10 minutes. Drain, transfer to a serving dish and drizzle over the remaining oil.

4 Add half the orange segments, half of the orange rind strips, the tarragon, and the fromage frais or ricotta cheese to the sauce in the pan and cook for 3 minutes.

5 Place the chicken on top of the pasta, pour over a little sauce, garnish with the remaining orange segments and rind, and the tarragon, and serve immediately.

Slices of Duckling with Pasta

A raspberry and honey sauce superbly counterbalances the richness of tender slices of duckling in this dish.

NUTRITIONAL INFORMATION

Calories 686   Sugars 15g
Protein . . . . 62g   Fat 20g
Carbohydrate . . . 70g   Saturates 7g

🄖 🄖 🄖

🍰 15 mins   🕐 25 mins

SERVES 4

I N G R E D I E N T S

4 boned breasts of duckling, about
   275 g/9½ oz each

2 tbsp butter

50 g/1¾ oz carrots, finely chopped

4 tbsp finely chopped shallots

1 tbsp lemon juice

150 ml/5 fl oz meat stock

4 tbsp clear honey

115 g/4 oz fresh raspberries, or frozen
   and thawed

3 tbsp plain flour

1 tbsp Worcestershire sauce

400 g/14 oz fresh linguine

1 tbsp olive oil

salt and pepper

TO GARNISH

sprigs of fresh flat-leaved parsley

fresh raspberries

1 Trim and score the duck breasts with a sharp knife and season well all over. Melt the butter in a frying pan, add the duck breasts and cook them until they are lightly coloured on both sides.

2 Add the carrots, shallots, lemon juice and half the meat stock and simmer over a low heat for 1 minute. Stir in half of the honey and half of the raspberries. Sprinkle over half of the flour and cook, stirring constantly, for 3 minutes. Season with pepper to taste and add the Worcestershire sauce.

3 Stir in the remaining stock and cook for 1 minute. Stir in the remaining honey and the rest of the raspberries and sprinkle over the remaining flour. Cook for another 3 minutes.

4 Remove the duck breasts and let the sauce simmer over a very low heat.

5 Meanwhile, bring a large saucepan of lightly salted water to the boil. Add the linguine and oil and cook for 8–10 minutes or until tender but still firm to the bite. Drain and divide between individual plates.

6 Slice the duck breast lengthways into 5-mm/¼-inch thick pieces. Pour a little sauce over the pasta and arrange the slices in a fan shape on top. Garnish with parsley and raspberries and serve at once.

Spicy Chorizo Vermicelli

Simple and quick to make, this spicy dish will set the taste buds tingling, with its wild mushrooms, chillies and anchovies.

NUTRITIONAL INFORMATION

Calories	672	Sugars	1g
Protein	16g	Fat	27g
Carbohydrate	90g	Saturates	6g

5 mins   10–12 mins

SERVES 6

INGREDIENTS

680 g/1½ lb dried vermicelli

125 ml/4 fl oz olive oil

2 garlic cloves

125 g/4½ oz chorizo, sliced

225 g/8 oz wild mushrooms

3 fresh red chillies, chopped

2 tbsp freshly grated Parmesan cheese

salt and pepper

anchovy fillets, to garnish

1 Bring a large pan of lightly salted water to the boil. Add the vermicelli and 1 tablespoon of the oil and cook until tender but still firm to the bite. Remove from the heat, drain and place on a large heated plate to keep warm.

2 Meanwhile, heat the remaining oil in a large frying pan. Add the garlic and cook for 1 minute. Add the chorizo and wild mushrooms and cook for 4 minutes, then add the chopped chillies and cook for 1 minute more.

3 Spoon the chorizo and wild mushroom mixture over the vermicelli and season with a little salt and pepper. Sprinkle over the freshly grated Parmesan cheese, garnish with anchovy fillets and serve the dish immediately.

VARIATION

Fresh sardines may be used in this recipe in place of the anchovies. However, ensure that you gut and clean the sardines, removing the backbone, before using them.

Spaghetti Bolognese

You can use this classic meat sauce for lasagne, cannelloni or any other baked pasta dishes.

NUTRITIONAL INFORMATION

Calories 732	Sugars 15g
Protein 39g	Fat 20g
Carbohydrate . . . 96g	Saturates 5g

5 mins   1¼ hrs

SERVES 4

I N G R E D I E N T S

3 tbsp olive oil

2 garlic cloves, crushed

1 large onion, finely chopped

1 carrot, diced

225 g/8 oz lean minced beef, veal
  or chicken

85 g/3 oz chicken livers, finely chopped

100 g/3½ oz lean Parma ham, diced

150 ml/5 fl oz Marsala

280 g/10 oz canned chopped
  plum tomatoes

1 tbsp chopped fresh basil

2 tbsp tomato purée

450 g/1 lb dried spaghetti

salt and pepper

1 Heat 2 tablespoons of the olive oil in a large saucepan. Add the garlic, onion and carrot and cook for 6 minutes.

2 Add the minced meat, chopped chicken livers and diced Parma ham to the pan and cook over a medium heat for 12 minutes until well browned.

3 Stir in the Marsala, tomatoes, basil and tomato purée and cook, stirring, for 4 minutes. Season to taste with salt and pepper. Cover the pan and simmer for about 30 minutes.

4 Remove the lid from the pan, stir and simmer for another 15 minutes.

5 Meanwhile, bring a large saucepan of lightly salted water to the boil. Add the spaghetti and the remaining oil and cook for about 12 minutes or until tender but still firm to the bite. Drain and transfer to a serving dish. Pour the sauce over the pasta, toss and serve hot.

VARIATION

Chicken livers are an essential ingredient in a classic Bolognese sauce, to which they add richness. However, if you prefer not to use them, you can substitute the same quantity of minced beef.

Pasticcio

A recipe that has both Italian and Greek origins, this dish may be served hot or cold, cut into thick, satisfying squares.

NUTRITIONAL INFORMATION

Calories 590	Sugars 8g	
Protein 34g	Fat 39g	
Carbohydrate ... 23g	Saturates 16g	

35 mins   1¼ hrs

SERVES 6

INGREDIENTS

225 g/8 oz fusilli, or other short pasta shapes

1 tbsp olive oil

4 tbsp double cream

sprigs of fresh rosemary, to garnish

SAUCE

2 tbsp olive oil, plus extra for brushing

1 onion, thinly sliced

1 red pepper, deseeded and chopped

2 garlic cloves, chopped

625 g/1 lb 6 oz lean minced beef

400 g/14 oz canned chopped tomatoes

125 ml/4 fl oz dry white wine

2 tbsp chopped fresh parsley

50 g/1¾ oz canned anchovies, drained and chopped

salt and pepper

TOPPING

300 ml/10 fl oz natural yogurt

3 eggs

pinch of freshly grated nutmeg

40 g/1½ oz Parmesan cheese, freshly grated

1 To make the sauce, heat the oil in a large frying pan and cook the onion and red pepper for 3 minutes. Stir in the garlic and cook for 1 minute more. Stir in the beef and cook, stirring frequently, until it is no longer pink.

2 Add the tomatoes and wine to the pan, stir well and bring to the boil. Simmer, uncovered, for 20 minutes or until the sauce is fairly thick. Stir in the parsley and anchovies and season to taste.

3 Cook the pasta with the oil in boiling salted water for 8–10 minutes or until tender. Drain and transfer to a bowl. Stir in the cream and set aside.

4 To make the topping, beat together the yogurt, eggs and nutmeg until they are well combined and season with salt and pepper to taste.

5 Brush a large, shallow, ovenproof dish with oil. Spoon in half of the pasta mixture and cover with half of the meat sauce. Repeat these layers, then spread the topping evenly over the final layer. Sprinkle the grated Parmesan cheese evenly on top.

6 Bake in a preheated oven, 190°C/375°F/Gas Mark 5, for about 25 minutes or until the topping is golden brown and bubbling. Garnish with sprigs of fresh rosemary and serve immediately.

Neapolitan Veal Cutlets

The delicious combination of apple, onion and mushroom perfectly complements the delicate flavour of veal in this recipe.

NUTRITIONAL INFORMATION

Calories	1071	Sugars	13g
Protein	74g	Fat	59g
Carbohydrate	66g	Saturates	16g

20 mins   45 mins

SERVES 4

INGREDIENTS

200 g/7 oz butter

4 veal cutlets, about 250 g/9 oz each, trimmed

1 large onion, sliced

2 apples, peeled, cored and sliced

175 g/6 oz button mushrooms

1 tbsp chopped fresh tarragon

8 black peppercorns

1 tbsp sesame seeds

400 g/14 oz dried tagliatelle

100 ml/3½ fl oz extra-virgin olive oil

2 large beef tomatoes, cut in half

175 g/6 oz mascarpone cheese

leaves from 1 sprig of fresh basil

salt and pepper

fresh basil leaves, to garnish

3 Melt the remaining butter in the pan. Cook the mushrooms, tarragon and peppercorns over a low heat for 3 minutes. Sprinkle over the sesame seeds.

4 Bring a saucepan of salted water to the boil. Add the pasta and 1 tablespoon of olive oil. Cook for 8–10 minutes or until tender but still firm to the bite. Drain and transfer to a plate. Keep warm.

5 Grill or fry the halved tomatoes with the basil for 2-3 minutes.

6 Top the pasta with the mascarpone cheese and sprinkle over the remaining olive oil. Place the onions, apples and veal cutlets on top of the pasta. Spoon the mushrooms, peppercorns and pan juices onto the cutlets, arrange the tomatoes and basil leaves around the edge and then place in a preheated oven, 150°C/300°F/Gas Mark 2, for 5 minutes.

7 Season to taste with salt and pepper, garnish with fresh basil leaves and serve immediately.

1 Melt 4 tablespoons of the butter in a frying pan. Cook the veal over a low heat for 5 minutes on each side. Transfer to a dish and keep warm.

2 Cook the onion and apples in the pan until lightly browned. Transfer to a dish, place the veal on top and keep warm.